#16

KAUFMAN BRENTWOOD BRANCH LIBRARY
11820 San Vicente Blvd.
Los Angeles, CA 90049

S0-BJQ-095

6 KAUFMAN BRENTWOOD

HOW TO DRAW LETTERING

Judy Tatchell and Carol Varley

Consultant: Graham Peet

Designed by
Nigel Reece and Richard Johnson

Illustrated by Fiona Brown and Guy Smith

Hand lettering by David Young

Additional illustrations by
Chris Smedley and Robin Lawrie

745.1 T216 1991

Contents

About lettering

Look around you and you see lettering everywhere. As well as in magazines, books and newspapers, it appears on shop signs, clothes, food wrappers and so on.

This book shows you how to design and do your own lettering. Below are some tips on how to choose a style that will suit your message.

Making a message clear

The most important thing about lettering is that it makes its message clear.

If a message is long or complicated you will need to use a simple style that is easy to read. Fancy styles are harder to read so they should be kept for short messages or greetings.

Books for young children need simple lettering that is easy to recognize.

It is harder to read this fancy lettering.

Choosing a style

A short message looks exciting and comes across well if you pick a lettering style that suits the message. Sometimes, the way the letters look can say almost as much as the words they form.

You can make letters look graceful...

...hurried...

...or technical.

You can combine letters with pictures.

Large or small?

Using very large or very small letters is a bit like talking loudly or softly. Messages that have to stand out and be noticed by passers-by need large, bold letters. This is like saying them in a loud, clear voice.

A poster has to grab people's attention – like a loud announcement.

Small lettering is more like normal conversation.

Using lettering

You can use lettering on cards, letters, projects, posters, T-shirts or just notes to friends. Later in the book, you can find out how to make several copies of your lettering using simple printing methods.

Notes

T-shirts

Labels

Cards

Tools and materials

Throughout the book there is information about paper, pens and materials you can use for lettering.

You can do most of the styles in this book with just colour pencils, felt-tip pens and watercolour paints.

Copying letters

You may like to copy some of the lettering you see in this book. These tips will help you draw the letters accurately. You need a sharp pencil.

The lines are called guidelines.

First draw some lines to help keep the lettering straight.

Keep your wrist still.

Sketch the outline of each letter. Let your wrist rest on the page and move only your fingers.

Use light strokes to sketch the letter.

Move your hand to a convenient position to draw each part of the letter.

Try to keep the outline smooth.

Go over the outline with a fine pen. You can leave it as it is or fill it in.

Lettering techniques

The following techniques help you to keep your letters the same size and in a straight line. You can use them with all kinds of lettering. They will help you to make the styles in this book look smart and professional.

Keeping letters even

You can keep your letters level and even by drawing faint pencil rules, called guidelines.

Unless you want very thin or very fat-looking letters, the distance between the guidelines should be between three and nine times the thickest part of your letter.

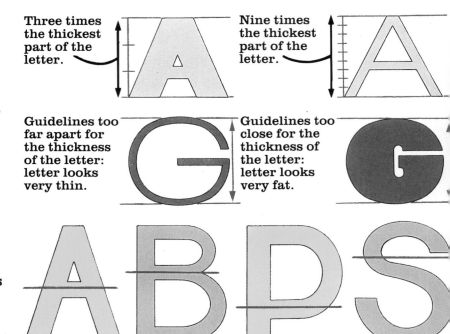

Three times the thickest part of the letter.

Nine times the thickest part of the letter.

Guidelines too far apart for the thickness of the letter: letter looks very thin.

Guidelines too close for the thickness of the letter: letter looks very fat.

Moving the middle

You can also draw a guideline to position the strokes across the middles of some letters. Moving this guideline up or down changes the look of the letters, as shown.

About pencils

Pencils are described by how hard or soft their leads are. The usual range is from 7B (softest) to 6H (hardest). A medium pencil is called HB. A 2B, an HB and a 2H are enough to start with.

A hard pencil makes a thin, greyish line. A soft pencil makes a thicker, blacker line which is easily smudged.

Hard pencils are useful for drawing faint guidelines. A softer pencil is probably better for sketching letter shapes.

Small letters

Small letters are just over half as tall as capitals. Small letter sticks (ascenders) and tails (descenders) extend above and below the guidelines by about the same amount. You can vary this for different effects, though.

Ascender

Capital letters also come up to this line.

baggy pants

Descender

Small letter guidelines.

Flowing letters

You can use an italic nib (see below) to do this flowing, joined-up style.

Try using just one guideline through the middle of the letters. It keeps them level but not absolutely even, so they look less rigid.

Try a single, curved guideline.

Spacing tips

Leave a space the size of a capital "E" between words made up of capital letters.

RRY E CHR

Leave the space of a small "n" between words made up of small letters.

cenuponnanti

About italic pens

For some of the styles in this book, you need a square-nibbed, or italic, pen. This gives a variety of thick and thin lines. You can find out more about italic writing on page 22.

You can put different italic nibs on a dip pen and use them with a bottle of ink.

You can buy felt pens with broad, flat italic-shaped ends from art shops.

To test whether you are holding the pen nib at the right angle, draw a cross. Both strokes should be the same thickness.

Hold the nib at this angle.

Atmospheric lettering

Some letters set a scene or create an atmosphere by their shape or the way they are decorated.

Decorating letters

The o, f, t and m on the right have all had their shapes adapted to help create an atmosphere. The s and the c have just been decorated. Colour also helps to give atmosphere.

Decorating letters is called illumination. You can find out more on page 20.

Hot. Red, orange and yellow are warm colours.

Cold. Icy blues and greens are cold colours.

Natural. The letter looks as if it is alive and growing.

Festive.

Marine. The outline ripples, like water.

Horrific.

Ancient letters

These letters look old and battered. You can get this effect by enlarging typed letters lots of times on a photocopier. A typewriter with a fabric ribbon produces the best results.

The letters break up as tiny faults get bigger and bigger. The more you photocopy them, the more aged the letters look.

These letters have been photocopied 20 times and enlarged 100% each time.

Metallic letters

Metallic letters look hard and stylish. Here, the position of the sparkle and highlights makes it look as if light is shining on the letter from the top left.

Sparkle
Highlight
Keep this area pale.
Bands of reflected colour.

Add the sparkle by flicking a sharp pencil away from the letter. Make two flicks join at a point.

Secret messages

A quick way to do lettering without doing it by hand is to use newspaper and magazine print. Here, different styles have been torn out roughly. This is supposed to resemble an anonymous message such as a kidnap ransom note.

You could use this sort of style for a joke. No one would expect a Valentine's Day message to be written in such a threatening style.

You can use whole words or make them up out of separate letters. Vary the size and style of the letters.

Digital style

This style makes a message look as if it might have come from a computer.

You could punch holes down the sides to make it look like computer print-out.

Most of the letters are made up from the same set of straight lines.

You have to make a few adjustments to prevent O looking like D, for example, or to complete Q.

Making an envelope

Put your card in the middle of a square of paper. There should be some space between the corners of the card and the paper's edges.

The paper needs to be strong but you must be able to fold it easily.

Fold each corner in round the card, one at a time.

Remove the card. Cut the triangles out where the folds cross (marked red).

Fold the bottom up and glue the sides to it.

Put your card inside. You can glue the top down or stick a cut-out shape over the join.

Time travel

You can give your letters a historical feel by copying the different styles people have used through the ages.

Gothic script

This style is based on a centuries-old script called gothic. Before printing was invented, books were copied out, usually by monks. They wrote in a style like the one below.

Gothic style has often been used for horror film and story titles. Above are some ideas for using a ghoulish gothic style.

In a creepy castle

You need a broad italic pen for this style. If you don't have one, try drawing the outlines of the letters and colouring them in. (There is a gothic alphabet to copy or adapt on page 30.)

The letters are squarish and angular. Small letters are made up of straight lines.

Capital letters are highly decorated.

Sampler lettering

An embroidered design made up of letters, numbers, pictures and words is called a sampler. This one was sewn by an 11 year old girl in 1760.

You can do letters which look as if they are made up of tiny stitches. Keep your crayons sharp or the "stitch" thickness will vary.

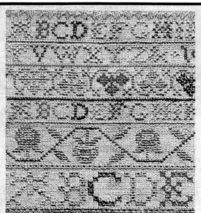

It is easiest to work on squared paper. Draw a letter outline in pencil, made up of straight lines. Fill it in with tiny crosses. Then rub out the outline.

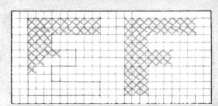

Art Nouveau

In the late 19th century, an artistic style called Art Nouveau developed. Art Nouveau lettering looks good when it is designed decoratively into a picture.

The letters below are natural shapes, like the trees. There is an Art Nouveau-style alphabet for you to copy or adapt on page 31.

Letters are designed into the picture and form part of it, rather than being added on top.

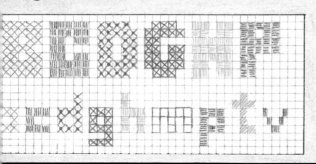

The letter shapes reflect the shape of the trees in the pictures.

1930s style

1930s design was elegant and precise. The shapes needed no decoration.

ABC 123

For capital letters in this 30s style, draw a simple letter shape. Thicken one side with downstrokes.

abcdefghi

Small letters have a round shape and a uniform thickness.

This style is good for short messages which need to be clear but stylish.

Here are some different stitch styles for you to try, and some ideas for pictures to go with them.

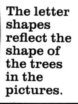

More lettering techniques

Here are some techniques that can make your lettering look very dramatic. They work particularly well with big, capital letters.

Letters in perspective

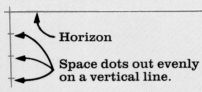

Horizon

Space dots out evenly on a vertical line.

Using a fairly hard pencil, such as a 2H, mark three dots on a vertical line. Then draw a horizon line further up the page.

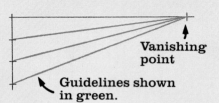

Vanishing point

Guidelines shown in green.

Mark a point on the horizon. This is called the vanishing point. Join each dot to it. Use the lines as your guidelines.

The upright lines remain vertical.

Do the letters closer together as they get further away.

Finally, rub out the guidelines.

Shadow lettering

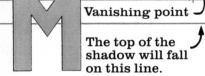

Vanishing point

The top of the shadow will fall on this line.

Draw the outline of a letter, a horizon and a vanishing point. Add a line where you want the top of the shadow to fall.

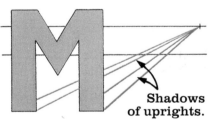

Shadows of uprights.

Draw lines from the uprights to the vanishing point. These lines show you where to position the shadows of the uprights.

Rub out the guidelines.

Use your judgement to position the other lines. Experiment until they look right.

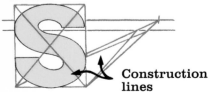

Construction lines

Curved letters are not easy. You can draw some extra lines, called construction lines, to help you.

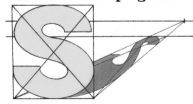

For the shadow, follow how the upright letter fits into its construction lines.

Letters in a word all go to the same vanishing point. You can rub out the letters and just keep the shadows.

Solid letters

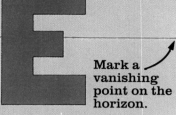

Mark a vanishing point on the horizon.

To make a letter look solid, first draw the letter outline. Then do a horizon just over half way up the letter.

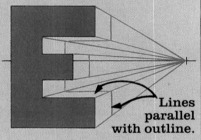

Lines parallel with outline.

Draw lines from the corners of the letter to the vanishing point. Then draw lines parallel with the letter's outline.

Rub out the guidelines for one letter before starting another. Colour the faces and bodies of the letter.

A word tower

This word tower is coloured like worn stone to make it look monumental. The steps below show you how to construct one like it.

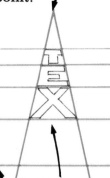

High vanishing point.

Guidelines showing letter heights.

Vanishing point on base line.

Construction lines

Darker colour for chips.

1. Draw a base line showing the width of the lowest letter. Mark a vanishing point in the middle of it. Mark another vanishing point high up, directly above it.

2. Draw guidelines from either end of this base line to the top vanishing point.

3. Draw guidelines to show the height of each letter. Letters get shorter as they get higher up. Then draw in the fronts of the letters.

4. To make the letters look solid, first draw lines from the corners and edges to the lower vanishing point.

5. Shade in the undersides of the letters. Do a letter at a time, ink in a chipped outline and rub out the construction lines. Colour a rough surface.

COMIC STRIP LETTERING

Looking at a comic strip is like a mix between watching a film and reading a story. A comic strip story is told partly in pictures and partly in words.

The lettering must be easy to read but it has several jobs to do. It shows what people say or think in bubbles. It contributes to the sense of drama and also provides sound effects.

The comic strip on these two pages contains examples of lettering used in all these ways.

Picture frames

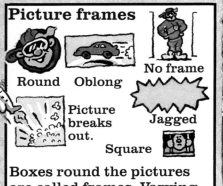

Round   Oblong   No frame

Picture breaks out.   Jagged

Square

Boxes round the pictures are called frames. Varying frame style keeps the strip lively. You can find all the frame styles above in the strip on the right.

You can draw the frames freehand. This gives your strip a relaxed look.

Comic strip titles

A title must stand out and suit the story. These styles and titles have been mixed up. Can you match the styles to the titles?*

*Answer: Dream Boy should be in the style of Space Station Alpha. Space Station Alpha should be in the style of Gas Street Gang. Gas Street Gang should be in the style of Dream Boy.

Sound effects

A sound effect is a kind of picture of a sound. There are several in the strip below. Here are some more to inspire you.

Speech bubbles

A speech bubble can show how words are said. For instance, small letters in a big bubble make words look quiet.

Centring letters

Speech bubbles look neat if you centre the letters. See below for how to do this.

Count the letters and spaces on each line:

Count fat letters such as w and m as three units.

Medium letters such as h, n and o are two units.

Spaces and thin letters such as i and t are one unit.

A capital letter has one extra unit.

Draw a vertical line. Put an equal number of units either side of it.

Use a thin black pen for the letters. Then draw a bubble outline around them.

People read from left to right, top to bottom. Position speech bubbles in the frame so that they will be read in the right order.

MAKING POSTERS

The most important thing about lettering on a poster is that it catches people's attention and is easy to read from a distance.

Materials

The size of the paper you use for a poster depends on how far away you want the poster to be seen from.

Poster for a notice-board.	A poster to go outside needs to be much bigger.

The lettering on a poster needs space around it. This will help the message to stand out. Make sure that the paper you choose is big enough for this.

Poster paper comes in different colours.

You can buy different kinds of paper from art shops. If your poster is going outside where it might get wet, buy a harder, less absorbent type of paper.

Use poster paint or gouache that does not run in the wet.

Designing a poster

First, write down what you want to say. Keep it simple.

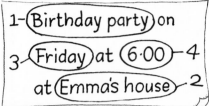

1 - Birthday party on
3 - Friday at 6·00 - 4
at Emma's house - 2

Then divide the message up and number the parts in order of importance. You need to make the most important words stand out.

Finally, choose a suitable style for the message and any illustration.

See opposite page for how to distort letters like this.

Drop shadows

To do a drop shadow, draw a letter. Then copy the outline a bit to the side, and above or below the letter shape. Fill in the shadow a darker shade.

Making letters bigger

If you want to copy small letters on to your poster, you can enlarge them to the right size using a grid.*

Draw a grid on tracing paper. Use about four squares to the height of the letter. Place it over the letter you want to copy.

Draw a larger grid on the poster the size you want the letter to be. Use a faint pencil line so you can rub the grid out later.

Copy what appears in each square of the small grid into the larger grid.

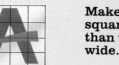

Squash and stretch

You can make the letters into strange shapes by distorting the grid.

Make the squares taller than they are wide...

...or wider than they are tall.

You could draw a wavy grid...

...or a curved one.

Poster tips

★ Use strong shapes and colours.
★ Don't use too many lettering styles and sizes on a poster or it will look confusing. Two or three different sorts is probably enough.
★ Attract people with a strong image and one main bit of writing. They will come closer to read the rest.

*You can use this technique the other way round, to make letters smaller.

Practising big letters

Practise big letters on old newspaper or large sheets of scrap paper. Do bold, wide sweeps of your hand.

Giant-sized posters

Billboard posters are made up of several sections. You could make a huge poster yourself, out of several sheets joined together.

Graffiti Styles

Graffiti styles look colourful and bold. The style developed when people began spraying their names on subway trains and walls in New York in the 1960s.

It is illegal to write graffiti on walls but you can use the style on paper. It makes a vivid splash.

Inventing a tag

A tag is a graffiti writer's signature. It is usually a nickname. You could invent a tag and use it instead of signing your name. It should be striking and easy to recognize.

NiGE

A tag needs to be quick to write. The quickest sort is one colour only.

BOZ-2

You could include your house number in your tag.

FLUR

This sort of tag is called a throw-up. It has an outline round a single colour.

Materials

Spray paints cover large areas quickly with flat colour. One way to copy this effect is to use marker pens. You can buy these from art shops. They are quite expensive, though, so you could try ordinary felt tips instead. The wider the tip, the better.

Marker pens

Graffiti masterpieces

Elaborate, highly-coloured, decorated bits of graffiti are known as "pieces", short for masterpieces. Here are some examples to inspire you.

This traditional style has overlapping bubble letters.

RAVIOLI

ELVIS

Graffiti is often painted on a cloud background.

Political graffiti

Sometimes people use graffiti for political or protest messages. It gets the message seen by lots of people but no one knows exactly who put it up.

This is Polish and means "solidarity".

Here are the logos of two political parties. It used to be illegal to belong to them. Graffiti styles suit the logos because members had to be secretive.

This stands for the Czechoslovakian party *Občanské Fórum* (Civic Forum).

This complex style has a pattern of interlocking letters which can be quite difficult to read. It is called wildstyle.

3-D graffiti letters stand out well from the background.

You could add some brilliant sparkles to some of the letters.

Some graffiti contains a cartoon character instead of a letter.

Graffiti technique

Good graffiti needs careful planning so sketch your idea in rough before doing the real thing on paper.

1. Roughly block out the letters.

2. Add a cloud background, scenery and decoration.

3. Work out the colour scheme and fill in the colours. Use bold colours to make it look like spray paint.

4. Add a firm outline both round the letters and round the whole piece.

17

Magazines and newspapers

You could make your own magazine or newspaper and photocopy it for your friends and family. It looks more convincing if the articles are typewritten or word processed.

You can make headlines and titles by cutting words out of real newspapers and magazines. The words in a headline need to be the same size and style. If you can't find all the words you can make them up out of separate letters.

AUTUMN SALE

RED SOX NEWS

VIDEO VIEW

Pets Corne[r]

Writing a news story

Newspaper stories grab your interest by telling a short version of the story in the first paragraph.

Then they go into more detail in the rest of the column.

Club member Di Hardy had a shock last week when she was fired from her Saturday job at Spotty's pet shop.

Proprietor Sam Spotworth caught Di setting mice free and smuggling a garter snake home in her pocket. Di told our reporter that the mice were overcrowded and that the snake looked ill. Red Sox have paid for the snake out of club funds. Most of the mice were caught and returned to Mr Spotworth.

Pictures

Photos and pictures help to break up the text so that it is not too dense or boring.

A colour picture will photocopy in black, white and shades of grey.

Typing columns

Justified columns in a newspaper.

Unjustified columns in this book.

Compare a newspaper with this book. The columns may look different. Columns with two straight sides are described as justified. You can justify columns on a typewriter as follows.*

Two extra spaces (one extra letter and one space between words).

Poppy Spike's film, B BANANA SKIN BLUES, is out on video. If you miss it, you are a ho hopeless head case.

One extra space.

Three extra spaces.

Set the typewriter to a width of, for example, 21 characters. Fill each line even if you do not have room to finish a word. This will show how much extra letter space each line has.

An extra space added between each of these words.

Poppy Spike's film, BANANA SKIN BLUES, is out on video. If you miss it, you are a hopeless head case.

One extra space added.

Three extra spaces.

Then type each line out again, adding the correct number of spaces between words to fill the whole line. Look at your first example to find out how many spaces to add to each line.

*Word processors can justify text automatically.

Laying out the pages

Newspapers and magazines are laid out on a plan, or grid. This has faint lines marking the columns. It keeps the pages neat.

1. Draw a grid, such as the one on the right, on a large sheet in pale blue or yellow. (This won't show up on a photocopier.)

2. Type your columns 2mm (1/10 in) narrower than the columns on the grid.

3. Plan where each article and picture will go. Cut the columns up and stick them down on the grid.*

The first paragraph of a story can spread over two columns. Then the story divides into two columns.

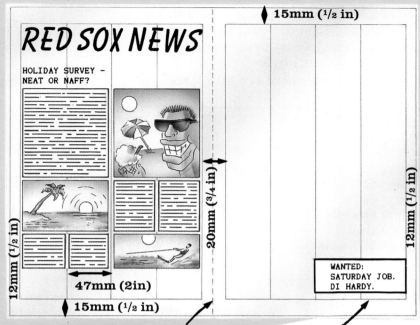

15mm (1/2 in)

RED SOX NEWS

HOLIDAY SURVEY – NEAT OR NAFF?

20mm (3/4 in)

12mm (1/2 in)

12mm (1/2 in)

12mm (1/2 in)

47mm (2in)

15mm (1/2 in)

WANTED: SATURDAY JOB. DI HARDY.

Paper will fold in half here.

Small advertisements or cartoons fill odd corners.

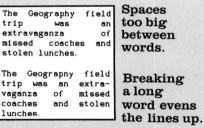

The Geography field trip was an extravaganza of missed coaches and stolen lunches.

Spaces too big between words.

The Geograpny field trip was an extra-vaganza of missed coaches and stolen lunches.

Breaking a long word evens the lines up.

If you end up with huge gaps between words, you can use a hyphen at the end of the line. Break the word where it is easy to read it. Don't do this more than once every few lines.

Copying the paper

Most photocopiers let you copy on to both sides of the paper. If you print on both sides of a large sheet and fold it in half, you end up with a four-page magazine or newspaper.

1. Paste up two sheets like this:

Back page 4	Front page 1

Page 2	Page 3

2. Photocopy pages 4 and 1.

Follow these stages so that the pages end up in the right order. Not all photocopiers behave the same so read the instructions and expect a few trial runs.

3. Put pages 2-3 in the copier ready for copying.

(4) (1)

4. Feed the copy of pages 4 and 1 in upside down and blank side up.

*The process of sticking the text and pictures on the grid is called paste-up.

Illuminating letters

In the Middle Ages, monks copying out books often decorated the first letter of a page or paragraph. This is called illumination.

Books were very rare and precious in those days. Monks used beautiful colours and even gold leaf to make the letters shine. You could do an illuminated letter at the beginning of a story or important message.

Boxed letters

Draw a faint box outline in hard pencil. Then sketch the letter outline inside.

You could colour the letter like this...

...or use details from a story.

Free letters

An illuminated letter can fill a whole page. You could make a card for someone by illuminating their initial. You could shape a message around it.

Modern styles

It is quite fun to mix this ancient technique with a modern lettering style. You could begin a letter to a friend with a big greeting.

Magazine style

Magazines often use a large initial letter to make a page look more interesting.

There is a gothic alphabet to copy or trace on page 30.

Tips

★ Try to make the letter as easy to read as possible.
★ The style of the rest of the writing should match the illuminated letter. Try gothic style if you want an ancient feel.*

Materials

A hard pencil is best for sketching decoration. You could use crayons, felt-tips or watercolour paint for colouring in.

You can buy gold and silver paint and pens from art shops. Metallic paint loses its shine with age, though.

Lettering on fabric

If you buy paints for fabrics, you can write on T-shirts, banners and flags.

Some fabric paints can only be used on natural materials such as cotton, so check the instructions. Check that the paint is washable, too.

T-shirt art

Bold, black letters on white T-shirts look very striking.

This style is often used for protest messages.

Work out your design on paper. Peg the T-shirt flat on a stiff board and copy the design in pale-coloured chalk. To do an exact copy, use the grid technique described on page 15. Now paint in the design. The chalk outline will soon wear off or wash out.

Practical tips

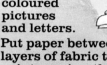

For crisp letter outlines, wear down the chalk to give it a sharp edge.

You could mix coloured pictures and letters.

Put paper between the layers of fabric to stop paint seeping through - not newspaper, though, as the print rubs off.

Printing on fabric

You can make fabric printing blocks using the techniques shown on pages 24-25. Use fabric paint or fabric printing ink, available from art shops.

You can repeat letter designs to create larger printed patterns.

Stretch the fabric out flat, as you did with the T-shirt.

Flags and banners

It is hard to read letters on flags so use short words. You could fly a flag outside on your birthday with your age on it. For longer messages, you could do lots of single letters across a stretch of bunting.

Try drawing a banner in miniature first. This makes it easier to work out the design. For example, if your banner is to be 3m (10ft) long, scale it down to 30cm (1ft). Use the grid technique (see page 15) to copy the design in chalk before painting it in.

Handwriting styles

Everyone's handwriting is different. It is as individual as your voice. Whatever its shape, though, it is important that it is easy to read. Some people practise handwriting as an art. This is called calligraphy.

The art of calligraphy

Calligraphy is based on traditional handwriting styles. Two calligraphy styles, roman and italic, are shown below.

Roman calligraphy has developed over 2000 years. It is upright, with rounded letters.

Italic writing was devised about 500 years ago. It slopes gracefully to the right.

Making large letters

You can draw large, italic style letter outlines using a twin-pointed pencil. To make one, tape two pencils tightly together.

The pencil points act like the edges of a nib.

Fill in the letters using a paintbrush.

Forming italic letters

Most italic letters are made up of several separate strokes. Take your pen off the paper between each stroke. Below are some letters to try. You can find out about italic pens on page 5 and there is an italic alphabet to copy on page 31.

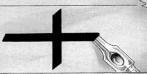

You will need to use a flat-tipped italic nib.* Hold it at the correct angle (see page 5).

Diagonal lines are thick or thin depending on which way your pen is moving.

Form rounded shapes in two separate strokes.

Arched strokes branch from about half way up the stem.

You need to do the pen strokes in the order and direction shown by the arrows.

Small finishing strokes are called serifs. To make these, push the pen up slightly before and after downward strokes.

For coloured calligraphy, try using either diluted poster paint or coloured inks.

*There are specially designed calligraphy

Another calligraphy style

Copperplate is a sort of italic style that was used for carving into glass or metal. On paper, people used quill pens which gave a thicker stroke when pressed harder.

You can try copperplate using any thin nib. Do continuous, sweeping strokes keeping the pen on the paper. You can thicken downstrokes afterwards.

Copperplate engraving on a silver tankard.

Letters flow into each other.

Swirls and flourishes

You can decorate calligraphy with flowing swirls, called flourishes. Here are some examples.

Make strokes in steady, continuous sweeps.

Pull the pen towards you for sloping lines.

Handwriting secrets

Some people believe that you can tell what a person is like from their handwriting. This is called graphology. Below are some of the things graphologists look for in handwriting.

Tall ascenders are supposed to show imagination.

grandly

Someone whose writing is very large in the middle area is supposed to be big-headed.

grandly

Big, curvy descenders may mean that a person is very athletic.

grandly

The slant of a person's writing is supposed to reflect their confidence.

Left slant: shy and private.

funny

Right slant: outgoing and sociable.

funny

Upright: self-controlled.

funny

If a person's writing slopes either up or down the page, this is supposed to indicate their mood.

Eager & enthusiastic

Tired and bored

You and your signature

To develop your signature, try writing your name very fast several times. Which bits feel easiest and how can you exaggerate them? Play with your signature like a design.

Some people think that your signature gives a clue to what you are like. Here are some signatures with different characteristics.

Romantic

Aggressive

Decisive

Printing letters

These two pages show you how to make printing blocks so that you can repeat your lettering again and again.

You could use this idea to make a personalized logo or your own slogan to use on cards and letters.

Making a printing block

You can make a printing block out of anything that is easy to carve, such as a lump of polystyrene or soft cork. You could make one out of a hard vegetable like a potato – but remember that a vegetable will go bad after a few days.

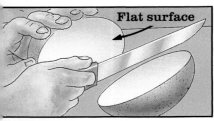

First, you need to cut the block so that it has a flat surface.

Draw a letter backwards on to the surface so it will print the right way round.

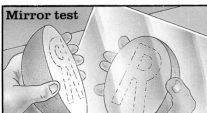

This is tricky so check the letter in a mirror before you cut it out.

Using a pointed knife, carve around the letter so that its shape is raised up. Cut out any spaces within the letter too.

Next, brush some paint or ink on to a flat plate. Press the printing block on to the paint to cover the surface of the letter.

Finally, press the block firmly on to the paper. Make sure the block does not slip sideways as this will smudge the letter.

Texture and colour

Printing blocks made from different materials can create unusual effects. You could experiment with different textures and coloured paints. Here are some ideas.

*Oasis is used for flower arranging. You can buy it from flower shops.

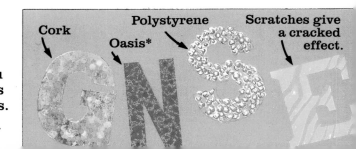

More printing blocks

Another way to make a printing block is to glue a letter shape on to a piece of wood. The surface has to be flat and the letter needs to be made out of something raised, such as string or corrugated cardboard.

Remember to draw letters in reverse and do the mirror test before you cut or glue.

Cut out the letter shape or form it out of string.

Glue the letter firmly on to the wood.

When the glue is dry, coat the letter with paint and print it (see opposite page).

Famous monograms

Yves
Saint Laurent

Volkswagen

Coco Chanel

Rolls Royce

Designs made out of letters are called monograms.
   Companies sometimes create monograms from their initials so that people will remember their names. Here are some famous monograms. You could try making a design out of your own initials.

Printed letter designs

By repeating letter shapes you can form intricate patterns and pictures.

Letter shapes

If you want to print a longer message, you can avoid cutting out every letter by making blocks for basic letter shapes.

Below are the four shapes you will need. You can combine them upside down and both ways round to make letters.

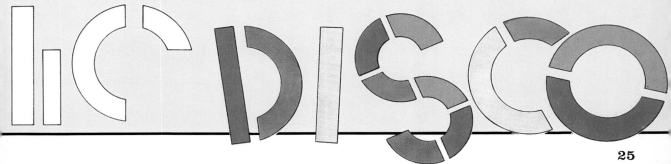

STENCILLING

Stencils are sheets of plastic or card with shapes cut out. You draw round or paint inside the shapes. You can create perfect lettering quickly and easily using a set of ready-made letter stencils. These come in various sizes.

Below are some different ways to use letter stencils.

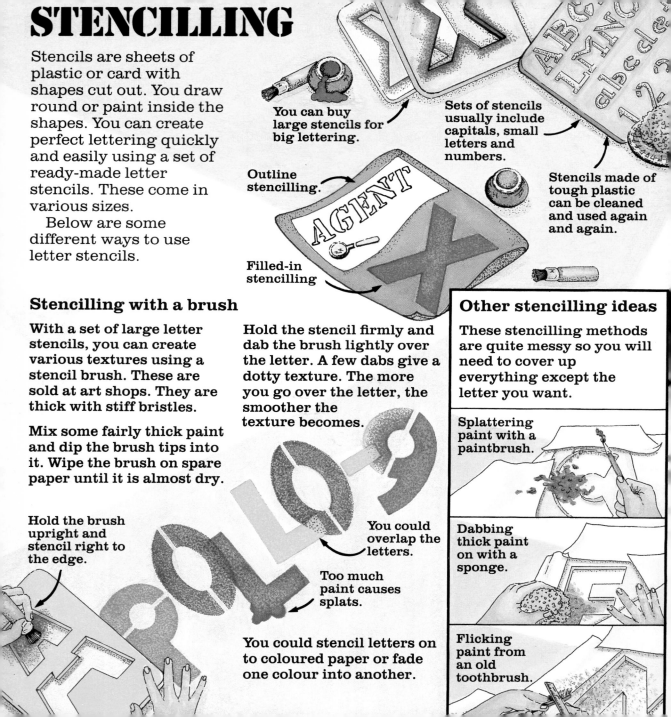

You can buy large stencils for big lettering.

Sets of stencils usually include capitals, small letters and numbers.

Stencils made of tough plastic can be cleaned and used again and again.

Outline stencilling.

Filled-in stencilling

Stencilling with a brush

With a set of large letter stencils, you can create various textures using a stencil brush. These are sold at art shops. They are thick with stiff bristles.

Mix some fairly thick paint and dip the brush tips into it. Wipe the brush on spare paper until it is almost dry.

Hold the brush upright and stencil right to the edge.

Hold the stencil firmly and dab the brush lightly over the letter. A few dabs give a dotty texture. The more you go over the letter, the smoother the texture becomes.

You could overlap the letters.

Too much paint causes splats.

You could stencil letters on to coloured paper or fade one colour into another.

Other stencilling ideas

These stencilling methods are quite messy so you will need to cover up everything except the letter you want.

Splattering paint with a paintbrush.

Dabbing thick paint on with a sponge.

Flicking paint from an old toothbrush.

Creative photocopying

Photocopiers are being used more and more by artists and designers. They can help you to create dramatic effects, correct mistakes and produce lots of copies of your finished lettering. Some can copy in colour.

Enlarging and reducing

Many photocopiers can make things larger or smaller. If you reduce lettering (make it smaller), smudges and wobbles become smaller too, so the letters look neater. By enlarging lettering you can make it look worn and patchy (see page 6).

Photocopiers enlarge or reduce by percentages. Many machines copy down to half-size (50%) and up to double size (200%). To make letters very big or small, you need to enlarge or reduce them many times.

Fancy lettering looks very precise if you reduce it.

You could do the last copy on to coloured paper.

3-D lettering

Modelling clay letters on the copier.

Using a photocopier, you can create flat lettering out of all kinds of solid objects. The copier copies shadows too, so the effect is 3-D. Because you see the back of the letters when you put them face-down on the copier, remember to form words back to front.

Multiple copies

If you are making cards or invitations, here is a quick way to make lots of copies.

Fold a piece of copier paper in four sections and do your lettering in one section.

Take a copy, cut it out and stick it next to the original.

Make a second copy and stick this underneath the first two.

You can use this master copy to print your hand-lettered invitations four at a time.

Correcting mistakes

To correct black and white lettering, stick a small piece of white paper over the error. Now take a copy and try again. If the patch shows, adjust the tone control for a lighter copy.

1. Error

2. Small patch.

3. Try again on a copy.

Layout and presentation

When information is well laid out and attractively presented, it is more enjoyable to read and easier to understand. These two pages give some advice on how you could present a school project. Many of the same tips are useful, though, whatever you are presenting.

Choosing your paper

Textured paper can clog up ink pens.

Patterned paper can make writing hard to read.

Some typewriters won't take thick paper.

Make sure your writing will show up if you use dark coloured paper.

Mistakes can be hard to correct on coloured paper.

Before you start writing up your project, you need to decide what paper to use. Bear in mind whether the project will be hand-written or typed: it needs to look clear and neat on the paper you use.

Introducing your project

The first pages of a document are called the "preliminaries". They should introduce the subject and make people interested in what they are about to read.

The cover should be eye-catching. It should display the title of the project and your name. You could add pictures which say something about the subject.

Next, there should be a list of contents. This should include all the sections in the project and give their page numbers. The title and contents list can go on the same page if you like.

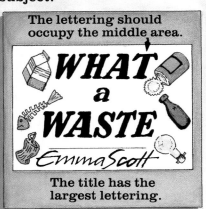

The lettering should occupy the middle area.

The title has the largest lettering.

Lettering should be smaller than on the cover.

WHAT a WASTE

Emma Scott.

A look at what we throw away and how to recycle it.

Brief description

The next page is the first page of your project. It is called the title page. Repeat the project's name and your own. You could also add a brief description of the project.

You could position the contents off-centre.

Contents

Make sure page numbers are not too far from their sections.

2
4
6
8
10
12
14
16

Laying out the pages

The layout of a page makes a lot of difference to how easy it is to read. An untidy or cramped page can be confusing.

Spaces make people pause and help them to absorb a piece of information before moving on to the next.

Headings have the largest lettering on the page. They introduce major new sections.

Sub-headings should stand out. They break the section into smaller topics and make it easier to absorb.

Leave plenty of space between lines and paragraphs.

Leave wide margins and generous spaces top and bottom of a page.

SPACE FLIGHT
Orbitting Satellites

Borders and motifs can add colour. Make sure they do not dominate the page though.

Illustrations should have lots of room. A large picture could have a whole page to itself.

Captions go underneath pictures or to one side.

Page numbers should be clear. The odd numbers go on the right hand page.

Ways to bind your project

You will need a binding to hold the pages of your project together. Take into account the number of pages and thickness of the paper when you choose a binding.

Ribbon can look elegant. Tie it quite loosely, though, or it will be hard to open the pages.

Cardboard at the back stops pages from getting crumpled.

A sheet of clear plastic protects the cover.

You could hold a small project together with staples.

You can protect punched holes with reinforcers from a stationery shop.

Around Our Town

You can have a project spiral-bound at a quick-print shop.

My Life So Far

You can buy slide binders from stationery shops

BATS

Alphabets to copy

Here are four alphabets for you to trace or copy. You can enlarge the letters using the grid technique explained on page 15.

Roman

ABCDEFGHIJKLM
NOPQRSTUVWXYZ
abcdefghijklmnopqrst
uvwxyz 1234567890

Gothic

ABCDEFGHIJKLM
NOPQRSTUVWXYZ
abcdefghijklmnopqrstuvwxyz
1234567890

Serif and non-serif alphabets

These four alphabets are serif alphabets, that is, the letters have finishing strokes. Letters without serifs, like those on page 4, are called sans-serif, or non-serif, letters.

Italic

*A B C D E F G H I J K L M
N O P Q R S T U V W X Y Z
a b c d e f g h i j k l m n o p q r s t u v
w x y z 1 2 3 4 5 6 7 8 9 0*

Art Nouveau

A B C D E F G H I J K L M
N O P Q R S T U V W X Y Z
a b c d e f g h i j k l m n o p q r s t u v
w x y z 1 2 3 4 5 6 7 8 9 0

Index

The photograph on page 8 is reproduced by permission of the Syndics of the Fitzwilliam Museum, Cambridge.

First published in 1991 by Usborne Publishing Ltd, Usborne House, 83-85 Saffron Hill, London EC1N 8RT, England.

Copyright ©Usborne Publishing Ltd 1991

The name Usborne and the device 🐝 are Trade Marks of Usborne Publishing Ltd.

All rights reserved. No part of this publication may be reproduced, stored in a retrieval system or transmitted in any form or by any means, electronic, mechanical, photocopying, recording or otherwise, without the prior permission of the publisher.

Printed in Belgium.   UE